WONDER CLEARING
DISCUSSION GUIDE

WONDER CLEARING
DISCUSSION GUIDE

_____

By Taylor Penfield

Foreword by Joy A. Barrett

RESOURCE *Publications* • Eugene, Oregon

WONDER CLEARING, DISCUSSION GUIDE

Resource Publications
An Imprint of Wipf and Stock Publishers
199 W. 8th Ave., Suite 3
Eugene, OR 97401

www.wipfandstock.com

PAPERBACK ISBN: 978-1-7252-8151-6
HARDCOVER ISBN: 978-1-7252-8150-9
EBOOK ISBN: 978-1-7252-8152-3

Manufactured in the U.S.A.   SEPTEMBER 15, 2020

This *Discussion Guide* is dedicated to the small group
that taught me, challenged me, and encouraged me.

"Connect, Respect, Revere, Care"

Contents

——

Foreword

_____

*W*onder is deeply embedded in the Judeo-Christian tradition as a dimension of faith. In the poetry of the Psalms and the poignancy of narrative, we are called to look around in awe and wonder at the beauty and diversity of all God's creation, to be curious and appreciative, to echo with the psalmist, "O Lord, our Sovereign, how majestic is your name in all the earth!" (Ps 8:9, NRSV)

In the book *Wonder Clearing* and in this companion *Discussion Guide* author Taylor Penfield opens the door to wonder, taking us on a journey that is life-changing and faith-deepening. I have the great privilege of serving alongside the author in the ministry of Christ in the congregation of Chelsea First United Methodist Church where I serve as pastor. Several members of our congregation have read and discussed the book. The participants readily shared how helpful it was to look through the lens of wonder in discussing potentially divisive topics. I echo those sentiments. Indeed, I believe that *wonder* is essential for creating civil society and beloved community.

In a time of extraordinary polarization—in national and world politics, in neighborhoods and families, in denominations and local churches—distrust and fear of the "*other*" too often rule the day. I have served as a United Methodist pastor over 35 years and as a delegate to the General Conference of our denomination eight times. I am keenly aware of the importance of respectful and heartfelt conversations about difficult matters. This *Discussion Guide* offers a framework to bring people together, centered in human stories, to cultivate a deeper capacity to wonder, discuss their differences, and still affirm care for each other.

Our congregation resonates with and affirms the themes of non-discrimination and inclusiveness without exception that are explored in *Wonder Clearing* and the *Discussion Guide*. I trust that this rich resource will be used in churches and groups to discover or rediscover the wonder and marvel of God and the wonder of one another.

Joy A. Barrett, Pastor
Chelsea First United Methodist Church
Chelsea, Michigan

Preface

——

Wonder Clearing is historically based fiction. The novel deals with issues of immigration, discrimination, sex, sexual orientation, disability, and misuse of power. The story offers small group participants a "novel" approach to discussing those issues and others. Just as Jesus used parables—stories—to teach about the Kingdom of God, the story of *Wonder Clearing* inspires group participants to revisit their own spiritual journeys.

Yes, participants will discuss their opinions and understandings about religious and political issues. But the story is not merely about issues that the characters faced from the 1950's into the twenty-first century. Nor is the story merely about how those issues have resurfaced in our current culture. Certainly participants will share their own interpretations of the Bible on current moral and political issues. Inevitably there will be stark differences of opinion. Then the main question of *Wonder Clearing* will face every member of the group: how can I treat people with whom I fervently disagree with respect and caring?

That is a question too much neglected. The idea of respecting and connecting with others who are outside our racial, national, socio-sexual, or creedal selves is revolutionary, counter-cultural, and counter-historical *and is precisely the way of Jesus.* Yet, through most centuries in the Common Era there has been an unbroken pattern of behavior among people claiming the name of Jesus of mistreating and even killing those who do not fit into their doctrinal, racial, or cultural patterns.

The questions facing those of us claiming the name of Jesus in our day are: will we continue the hostile and sometimes violent ways of the past or will we return to the blessed life of early believers in living more consistently mercy, compassion, and reconciliation? That blessed life can be discovered or rediscovered in and through the wonder of God's love for all people. The discussion guide offers questions and Scriptures for group members to explore as they prayerfully seek God's guidance to follow the way of Wonder: "to connect, respect, revere, and care."

Acknowledgments

————

In the process of writing the novel, *Wonder Clearing*, a number of readers reviewed the draft. One of those readers was the Reverend James Nenninger. Jim is a retired Clinical Pastoral Education Supervisor. He saw the possibility of using *Wonder Clearing* for discussion groups in churches. After I moved to Chelsea, Michigan, my wife and I started to attend a fabulous church called Chelsea First United Methodist Church. The pastors there, Joy Barrett and Rodney Gasaway, encouraged me to facilitate a group.

This group's charge was not only to discuss the book but also to help me develop a discussion guide for other churches. The group met for six sessions in the fall of 2019. Each week one of the participants would act as the scribe to record group interactions. Those scribal notes and my own notes were utilized in formulating this *Discussion Guide*. I remain grateful to the members of this group. Particular appreciation goes to four members of the group who have allowed me to share their stories: Christin Bieber, Barbara Brown, Bev Dronen, and Sandy Schmunk.

ACKNOWLEDGMENTS

I also remain grateful to the pastors, staff, and administration of Chelsea First United Methodist Church for graciously assisting me and encouraging me in the development of this discussion guide. Of course my warmest appreciation goes to my wife, Eunice Peters; she was and is my supporter and helper. In this endeavor her review and comments have been especially helpful.

Prologue through Chapter 5

———

SUMMARY

From reflections at Alphonso's (Al's) funeral Mass, Rob (Bobby) tells his readers: " . . . our calling was about more than living our personal creeds. It was a boyhood call to be in awe at the mystery of the God of many names. It was a summons to stand resolutely against hate and misunderstanding."

It is that summons that Bobby's Grandpa heeds after his disillusionment with the prejudice and violence of the Ku Klux Klan. It is that summons that Bobby and Al live out in their growing up years in a town that welcomed only families that were "White and Protestant."

Economic necessity means a dire need for an exception to the rule of "White and Protestant." A Catholic immigrant family, the Basilones, comes to live in Steepleton where they receive tolerance but not acceptance.

Bobby rescues, Alphonso, a son of that family from bullies. Immediately after that forest rescue, Bobby and Alphonso experience the wonder of a shaft of light from a stormy sky; wonder then builds in them as a full rainbow and a flight of doves appear above them.

But the thrill of that wonder is dashed with a bullying prank of "yellow dresses" at school. Then their mothers become involved; the bullying prank becomes an entrée to friendship of the families and musical comradeship for Bobby and Alphonso.

Before the first session please read the Prologue through Chapter 5 in *Wonder Clearing*. Then jot down notes on the following:

Has an experience of wonder in childhood had a lasting effect in shaping your life? If so, describe (e.g., camps, experience of nature, or the self-sacrifice of a friend).

—Read Genesis 37: 3–11 and Matthew 19:14.

Does your community find ways to keep people of different races, religions, or cultures from coming to live in your community? How can you make your community more welcoming?

—Read Exodus 22:21 and Matthew 9:10–13.

Are there people living near you who may feel tolerated but not accepted? If so, what can you do to show them acceptance and caring?

—READ JAMES 2:8–9.

Bobby and Al believed that God had planned Al's rescue. Do you believe in the personal, protective care of God? If you do believe in God's protective care, why? If not, why not?

—READ PSALM 23 AND JOHN 10:25–30.

"Pranks meant to demean two pre-teen boys had brought two very different families together." How can community response to school bullying encourage caring and understanding?

—READ HEBREWS 13:1–2; MATTHEW 25:35.

Alphonso was able to become a talented violinist because of the generosity of a benefactor. What opportunities have come your way because of the generosity of others?

—READ PHILIPPIANS 4:10–20.

VIGNETTE:
Barbara's Story

I grew up on the south side of Chicago in an Italian/Polish neighborhood that was predominantly Catholic. Within three blocks of my home, there were two Catholic churches and schools. Both had marvelous carnivals each summer honoring their patron saints. Next to Christmas and birthdays, the carnivals were highlights of our year. We enjoyed Italian lemonade, sausage sandwiches, rides, games, fireworks, parades, and "bombs" that went off every night. The Methodists had nothing to compare with this!

Often on Saturday afternoons, I would accompany Cathy, my next-door neighbor, when she went to confession. While I sat in the back of the church, she would walk up to the confessional, discuss the sins she had committed during the past week, kneel at the altar, and say her Hail Marys and Our Fathers. As we left the church, I envied Cathy because she was leaving free of sin and I was still a guilty Methodist.

Barbara Brown, Chelsea Group Participant

4

Why are attitudes of prejudice and discrimination prominent in some places and not in others? What gives people who are racially, culturally, or religiously different the ability to relate in positive ways with each other?

—READ JOHN 4:1–30.

Other issues or questions that I would like to discuss at the first group session:

Chapters 6 through 10

SUMMARY

Bobby and Al want to make sense of their "wonder" experience. They cannot find proper rational explanations. They turn instead to what they knew and felt in their "wonder" moments. That experience had brought them to a deep, sensitive awareness—of presence, of relationship, of creation, of direction, and friendship. They want explanation; instead the Wonder maker calls them " . . . to connect with people, to respect others and [themselves], to revere the marvel of life and living, and to care deeply for people and for the world within which [they] lived."

Molly, Bobby's sister, is a girl with Down syndrome. When she becomes lost in the forest, Shep, the family dog, and Al rescue her. Molly in the years ahead always seemed to be emotionally in tune with others. Rob remembers:

"As in her living, in her final hours of dying she showed such empathy and kindness toward her family."

Bobby and Al present a concert for their families at the Bernardo Memorial Mansion. Both families bond in their appreciation of the music and in their common abhorrence of the bullying of Steepleton. Issues of the use or non–use of alcoholic beverages and their separate religious loyalties divide them. Rob shares the story of how Bobby and Al in a visit to Wonder Clearing " . . . talked explicitly about [their] teen sexual struggles."

In high school Al falls in love with a beautiful Irish girl named Jacqueline. Her parents do not want her to date an Italian. They consider Italians to be " . . . lazy, dirty, and immoral." Al demonstrates his pugilistic skills in defending himself at school. Bobby is told by his mother not to go into the sanctuary of a Catholic Church. He secretly disobeys and confesses: "I was totally not at peace."

Bobby and Al talk about Bobby's discomfort in the Catholic sanctuary. At the insistence of her parents, Al and Jacqueline reluctantly agree to date others at their colleges. A conniving fraternity brother, Larry, misidentifies himself as the son of a famous Irish politician. He dates Jacqueline and eventually rapes her. She becomes pregnant. She goes home and tells her parents. They do not believe her. They are sure that an honorable Irishman like Larry would not molest her and are sure that Al is the guilty party. They call Jacqueline a "whore." Upset, she drives too fast and dies in a car accident. Her sister, Marg, confronts the rapist.

Before the second session please read Chapters 6 through 10 in *Wonder Clearing*. Then jot down notes on the following:

Can the wonder of our faith be buried with analysis? How? Why?

—READ ECCLESIASTES 8:16–17 AND 1 CORINTHIANS 2:11–13.

Molly was emotionally in tune with others; she had a high EQ—Emotional Intelligence. Who in your life models emotional intuition and connection with others?

—READ LUKE 10:38–42 AND MATTHEW 26:6–13.

How can the Christian community provide positive guidance to youth as they face normal teen sexual struggles?

—READ PROVERBS 22:6; 1 TIMOTHY 4:11–16.

How can preconceived attitudes about others hurt our ability to connect and respect?

—READ JOHN 1:44–46.

VIGNETTE:

Sandy and Christin

Sandy is stately in demeanor and height. Her works of compassion and caring—her literal feeding of the hungry—are well known. She did not speak from the realm of lofty ideas and ideals—although she had studied many of them well. She shared from the heart of a retired social worker, a mom, and a grandmother. We had just talked about the rape of Jacqueline. Sandy spoke up and said: "I saw a sign in front of the Catholic Church: 'End abortion.' I wanted to add: 'End rape' . . ."

Sitting beside her was an attractive young woman, Christin. She is a mother of three children—one of whom had been adopted. She could not be flippant about the treatment of women and children. She had seen too much pain in the eyes of unwanted and neglected children. She knew too well the long history of women being treated as things to be used and misused. Too many women had been left to raise children alone and in poverty. In tandem with Sandy's words, she added: "End childhood poverty . . . And together they added: "End abuse" and then "End shame."

From comments of Sandy Schmunk and
Christin Bieber, Chelsea Group Participants

Both those against and those for choice see themselves as caring for and about infants; what Scriptures and spiritual understandings support your position on abortion?

—READ EXODUS 21:22–23 AND MATTHEW 18:10.

Other issues or questions that I would like to discuss at the second group session:

Chapters 11 through 15

————

SUMMARY

Al and Rob are sure "that the experience of awe is a part of human DNA." But they also find that the 'wonder' gene is not " . . . equally dominant in all people." Al tells his family about his intention to enter a seminary toward becoming a priest; he fears that he will lose his violin. Instead he discovers family support and a supportive Codicil in the Bernardo Trust.

Al's brother Martino becomes a football star on the Steepleton football team. He realizes that he is cheered for helping the team; but he still experiences discrimination as an Italian immigrant's son. Martino is killed in Viet Nam. Al is again overwhelmed with grief. Rob remembers his own collegiate struggles with " . . . the real issues of living a life of faith under the brightness of the love of Jesus."

Rob meets Julia at a dance. He fears dating a nursing student. His dominant nurse mother had ruled his family and bullied his father. After seeing the movie *One Flew Over the Cuckoo's Nest*, he had told Julia: "'Nurse Ratchet, Nurse Helen, the same.'" Years later riding with his mother in the funeral limousine after his father's burial, he learns the rest of the story and concludes: " . . . not the same, different, loving, and caring, a gift to Dad—a gift to me."

Rob raises money to buy a car by working as a salesman. He takes Julia to a popular "parking" spot near the college. He presses Julia for sexual intimacy. She tells him her father's World War II story to argue for waiting until marriage and ends her argument with a question: "'Don't you think I'm worth waiting for?'" Julia becomes Rob's advisor on other current social issues.

Al and Rob talk about the differences in the discernment processes for clerical vocations in their two different religious traditions. Al takes issue with political dimensions and psychological testing in Rob's processes. Both men later in their ministries stress both spiritual discernment and psychological evaluation for ministerial candidates.

Before the third session please read Chapters 11 through 15 in *Wonder Clearing*. Then jot down notes on the following:

VIGNETTE:

Sensitivity to Wonder

Al's next letter asked an interesting question: "Why are you and I so aware of the call of wonder to care and respect?" He wrote:

I suppose one answer is Wonder Clearing. But what if I were a [strictly doctrinaire] Catholic and you a [strictly doctrinaire] Protestant? When we were in that forest that memorable day, would we have paid more than momentary attention to our wonder experience? I think we both would have quickly given a nod to what we saw, heard, and experienced. Then we would have returned to the explanations of our traditions.

I come from a part of the Roman Catholic Church long accused of being focused on magic. I think parts of my tradition did tend to talk about magic—witches, ghosts, and spells. However, I think behind all that was a sense of the awesome— of mystery. My sensitivity to mystery and marvel is ingrained in me as an Italian American.

From an earlier unpublished version
of *Wonder Clearing*

Do you agree with the Master Class violin teacher and Einstein about the universality, necessity, and humanizing experience of Wonder? Why do some people seem more sensitive to the experience of wonder?

—Read Proverbs 9:10–12; Acts 2:42–44

Rob and Al were opposed to the Viet Nam War. At the same time both felt guilt that other men served in their places. How does opposing war or a particular war fit in with the call to discipleship?

—Read John 18:36; Matthew 8:5–13; Acts 10:1–2.

How can the church community become more accepting of people with mental illness?

—Read Ephesians 4:2–6; Romans 12:9–16.

Jesus by example and words detested the objectification of women. How do dating customs in our culture conform or not conform to the high standards of Jesus in valuing the personhood of men and women?

—Read John 8:3–11.

Can secrecy be used for both good and evil?

—Read Proverbs 11:13, Matthew 26:15–17, and 2 Peter 2:1–3.

Other issues or questions that I would like to discuss at the third group session:

SESSION 4

Chapters 16 through 20

SUMMARY

Al is called to the Bronx Veteran's Hospital to meet Marty's seriously wounded commanding officer, Benyamin (Bennie) Cohen. Al's experience of walking the halls of that hospital affirms Bennie's assessment: " . . . the worst excuse for care for Vets . . . " Al sees Marty's leather bag; Al knows that it contains Marty's mission rosary.

In a special moment of "confidential togetherness" Benyamin meets with Al. He tells Al that both his Magen David and Marty's mission rosary symbolized their determination "' . . . to protect and defend helpless people.'" Bennie tells the story of the battle where Marty died and he was wounded. Bennie somberly presents the mission cross to Al.

In separate seminaries Al and Rob become indoctrinated in the fine points of their theologies. In letters they fight " . . . each other with doctrines, church history, tradition, and occasionally the teachings of Jesus." Their relationship suffers and briefly ends.

Julia issues an ultimatum to Rob: reconcile with Al or lose her. After a late night phone call from Al, they agree to meet at the Circle Diner. Al senses from their phone conversation that Al had concerns about sex. As Al enters the restaurant, a rock love song blares from the juke boxes. Al shares his embarrassing history with that particular love song and the Circle Diner. They roar with laughter. As Rob put it, "The ice was broken. We could talk and talk we did."

Rob and Al find reconciliation with each other and misunderstanding of their relationship with the waitstaff. They become very clear about their disagreements and sometimes learn " . . . from each other." As they envision their future ministries, they determine to be frank about their different views without breaking their relationship.

Before the fourth session please read Chapters 16 through 20 in *Wonder Clearing*. Then jot down notes on the following:

VIGNETTE:

Keepers and the Kept

To be fair, there were a lot of caring people at the Bronx VA Medical Center. There was, however, the lethargy of institutionalization. Some staff members were easily inured to the concerns of those they were to be serving. There was a kind of depersonalization that happened almost unconsciously with many staff members. Somehow it was easy to consider the wounded and sick veterans as less

human than they were. This was the classic phenomenon of the keepers and the kept. Some of
the staff, however, refused to be caught up in this
phenomenon. They saw themselves, their broth-
ers, fathers, and cousins in the eyes of those they
served. They desperately fought for proper care and
attention to the patients.

From an earlier unpublished version
of *Wonder Clearing*

What is our duty as Christians when institutions fail vulnerable people?

—Read Ezekiel 34:1–6 and Matthew 25:34–36.

Al, Rob, Bennie, and Marty had experienced discrimination and hate but they chose to protect and care for vulnerable people. What motivated them to care for others
and what motivates you to care for others?

—Read James 1:27, Colossians 3:12–13, and 2 Corinthians 1:3–4.

How or why do the teachings of Jesus get lost in arguments?

—Read Ephesians 4:31–32, Matthew 7:12, and Gala-
tians 5:22–23.

Julia asks Rob: "And just what sophisticated new information has suddenly changed your respect for Al?" Can sophistication, academically, Biblically, or theologically, be detrimental to simple acceptance and caring for people who have different ideas or opinions?

—Read 1 Corinthians 13:2–7, Philippians 2:3, and Romans 12:3.

Since from their point of view Al was only stating facts in his letter to Rob, why would Father Charles challenge Al about the letter?

—Read John 15:17, 1 Corinthians 13:1, and 1 Peter 3:8–9.

Other issues or questions that I would like to discuss at the fourth group session:

SESSION 5

Chapters 21 through 25

SUMMARY

Al and Rob are challenged with issues of clergy sexual misconduct. Rob deals with those issues and his judgmental tendencies in Clinical Pastoral Education. He is shocked at the detrimental effects of rigid religious teachings on a psychiatric patient.

Rob is teamed with a senior pastor, Pastor Steve, at a growing vibrant church called Doright United Methodist Church. Pastor Steve misuses his power to sexually misuse women. After Pastor Steve is transferred to another church, the congregation and fellow clergy accuse Rob of not defending Pastor Steve.

Al visits Rob at Doright. In a Pocono Mountain clearing, Al tells Rob: "The very worst days of our lives can be the best days." He reminds Rob that "Living the mission of wonder . . . will not be easy. But then: 'Wonder won. Wonder wins.'"

Rob is appointed to a three point circuit nicknamed "BBC Horror." Julia speaks up at a church conference and ends the reign of the church boss. The three churches of the circuit merge to become the Unity United Methodist Church. Communing people at a nursing home convinces Rob that communion was a "'not often enough element'" in the life of the church. After being told that Pastor Steve had again been "'overly comforting'" to young widows, Julia is troubled by his new assignment in a seminary with vulnerable co-eds.

Al serves as the pastor of a Catholic church near Philadelphia. He continues to be concerned " . . . about the way the Catholic Church [is] handling the pedophile priest issue." Rob visits Al. Al tells him about the long history of the misconduct of priests with women and children. Al points to a prominent issue in clergy misconduct in his church and Rob's: clerical power. Even at risk to his career Al speaks out in the Diocese for more effective handling of sexual abuse accusations.

Before the fifth session please read Chapters 21 through 25 in *Wonder Clearing*. Then jot down notes on the following:

VIGNETTE

Harm in the Name of Religion

The scribe for the session had heard the group discuss this question. But there it was for me in black and white in the scribe's notes: "How much harm do we do in the name of religion?" That question has haunted me at every stage of my ministry.

There may be some solace in Rob's words:

I know now that Dr. Jerry's summary was overly simplistic. Usually rigid religious teaching does not cause mental illness. Instead some people because of brain chemistry, heredity, or other factors may be predisposed to mental illness. As they become mentally ill, they may latch on to negative religious teachings and religiously oriented distortions of reality.

Edited quote from an earlier unpublished version of *Wonder Clearing*.

Personally I find little solace in those words; I find instead an even harsher, more personal question: What have I done in words and actions in ministry through the years that has been a catalyst not for healing but for a "somebody" or "somebodies" to fall into the abyss of mental illness? There is a more positive ancillary question too: What have I done in words and actions to bring comfort and support to people who must deal with serious mental challenges every day?

The questions are not just for those of us who are officially called ministers. All Christians are to serve in ministries; so the hard and harsh question and the question of support and caring are for all of us.

What are we doing in words and actions in the Christian community that may be a catalyst for a "somebody" or "somebodies" to fall into the abyss of mental illness? What are we doing in words and actions to bring comfort and support to people who must deal with serious mental challenges every day?

—Read Romans 8:22–25 and Hebrews 13:1–3.

Have you or someone you know been a victim of clergy sexual misconduct? How would you want the church to respond to alleged victims?

—READ MICAH 6:8, MATTHEW 23:23, AND 2 CORINTHIANS 4:7–12.

Rob wrote: "Winning was then for both of us and is still for me living courageously in harmony with wonder." What are your thoughts about the motto: "Wonder Won; Wonder Wins"?

—READ LUKE 6:35 AND LUKE 17:33.

Rob described the worship of the new Unity United Methodist Church: "The focus of every service became as you might expect the wonder of connection with God and each other and the privilege of caring about each other and our world." What are your thoughts on the focus for worship?

—READ ACTS 2:43–45.

Al told Rob: "The problem is 'Power corrupts and absolute power corrupts absolutely.'" How can power tempt us to take our eyes away from caring and valuing others?

—READ MARK 10:42–45.

Other issues or questions that I would like to discuss at the fifth group session:

SESSION 6

Chapters 26 through 30

————

SUMMARY

Al tells Rob about a gathering in his church called "Molly's People"; the gathering, Father Al explains, "' . . . is for people with disabilities; that means all of us. We share our abilities in support of each other.'" Al's Auxiliary Bishop has nightmares about children being abused by clerics. In his dream, Holy Mary tells him: "'In the name of my Son and your Lord, protect my precious little ones.'" He struggles with following the dictates of his church and listening to his dream. Al becomes the Director of Social Services for the Archdiocese.

At his new appointment at Sanland, Rob marvels at the " . . . heightened sense of awe for [his] congregation when people with obvious intellectual disabilities reverently receive communion." He admits to a marital crisis during his early years at Sanland. A counselor confronts him about his "'emotional infidelity,'" self-absorption, and self-deception.

Obvious close friendship and embraces between Rob and Al at a dinner meeting at a Hotel in Philadelphia are misinterpreted; an unnoticed observing Monsignor concludes that Rob and Al are Gay lovers. Julia goes with Al and Rob to meet with Diocesan investigators of the scandal. Julia concludes her defense of Al and Rob with: "'Investigate all you want. You will find two men of character whose pure friendship has been based on their mutual yet different friendship with God.'"

After an affair with a nun Al asks to be assigned to a mission church in the "Badlands" of Philadelphia. He becomes part of a "God–Allah Squad" made up of an Imam, a charismatic preacher, and Father Al. Together they provide tangible supports to the people of " . . . the hardest and most dangerous parts of the Badlands neighborhoods."

A failed terrorist bombing attempt at the Philadelphia Eagles' Football field, leads to a rumor of the association of the "would be" terrorists with the Imam's mosque. A radio sports announcer leads a mob of football fans in a caravan to the mosque. The three interfaith clerics of the "God–Allah Squad" stand together in front of the mosque; they are spotlighted by the headlights of cars of the caravan. Al lifts his violin to his shoulder and soothes the crowd with "The beauty of the melody of Beethoven's Spring Sonata . . . " Al is shot. His last words are: "'Wonder won.'"

Session 6: Chapters 26 through 30

Before the sixth session please read Chapters 26 through 30 in *Wonder Clearing*. Then jot down notes on the following:

"And Vilardi understood well the message. It was not: 'Stop the abuse.' It was: 'Protect the Church and its reputation.'" Have you ever struggled with an issue of doing right and acting with integrity and compassion with your job, your life, or livelihood at risk? If so, describe the situation and your decision.

—Read Joshua 24:14–16, Esther 4:9–14, and John 18:15–27.

VIGNETTE

Bev Dronen

She is a good neighbor and friend. She was there for us when my wife faced surgery. She served as one of the scribes at the group discussion sessions. At every session she was so very supportive and insightful—until the very last session. Actually there were times in other sessions that I wondered: "How did this mild mannered, considerate, soft spoken person survive as a doctor?" But in that last session I learned the hard way: "This woman is no pushover."

Dr. Dronen took strong exception to the ease of Rob's departure from loyalty to Julia to nursing his own hurts. With an "in my face brashness" Bev let me know: Rob should have been called to account in the novel for his insensitivity and self-absorption.

Rob had lots of reasons to empathize and support Julia—not necessarily on particular issues always—but always in support of her as a person. Even when Pastor Steve sexually harmed her, Julia had sacrificially supported Rob and cared for him. Throughout his career, she had continually been Rob's strong advocate. In supporting Rob and in advocating for vulnerable women she had shown strength of character, compassion, and loyalty.

In an email Bev apologized to me: "I think I was a little brash last night and want to apologize for my behavior." I answered: "Your apology is accepted but your insights are treasured."

At the group session, Bev had expressed it well, "Rob was a 'wiener.'" And for his behavior in that section of the book, I failed to properly identify him as an insensitive, self-absorbed wimp.

Taylor Penfield with input from Bev Dronen

Has insensitivity, self-deception, or self-absorption ever kept you from valuing someone close to you? How do you or how can you keep your focus on the treasure of a close relationship?

—READ PSALM 51 AND EPHESIANS 5:25–33.

Al and Sister Margaret are described as having " . . . an open, accepting, and loving attitude toward people of differing sexual orientations." What is your Biblical/

theological reasoning for inclusion or exclusion of persons of differing sexual orientations in the full life of the church?

—Read 2 Corinthians 13:11 and Ephesians 4.

The Imam told Rob: "'I believe we have a common command to love our neighbors and to care for the poor and the hurting.'" Can focus on service and caring help to unite people of different religions?

—Read Luke 10:25–37 and James 2:14–26.

Rob writes about the two "would be" terrorists: "Their beloved family members had become part of the underreported tens of thousands of civilians killed in the US military campaign." There is a continuing cycle of violence between nations and persons. How can we be peacemakers?

—Read Matthew 5:1–12, Matthew 5:38–39, and James 3:17–18.

Other issues or questions that I would like to discuss at
the sixth group session:

Agent of Wonder

———

1. You have been chosen to be an agent of Wonder. Your leadership of the group will indeed include encouraging the expression of differing points of view on important ethical and moral issues. But your major role will be to guide the group back from divergent points of view to the unity of the way of Wonder: "to connect, respect, revere, and care."

2. At the first session and in advertising the group, acknowledge that the group is an opportunity to share ideas and opinions on current ethical and spiritual issues. The teachers for the sessions are the participants.

3. You may want to introduce each session by summarizing the content of the assigned chapters. The brief summary of the chapters in the *Discussion Guide* may be read or you may want to ad lib your own summary.

4. While there is one question in the *Discussion Guide* for each chapter, there are many issues related to following Jesus in each chapter. After summarizing the chapters for the session, you may want to ask participants to share other issues or questions noted by participants.

5. Encourage group members to read the assigned chapters and to answer the *Discussion Guide* questions before coming to the discussion group.

6. Have someone serve as a "scribe" in each session to record issues discussed and meaningful moments in each session. Share the notes with participants by email in between each session.

7. Be punctual: begin and end on time.

8. Honor the Wonder Maker and seek direction by beginning and ending the group discussions with prayer.

9. Encourage participants to honor the wonder of each other. Unity will be found not always in agreement but always in the mystery and marvel of being part of the body of Christ.

10. Acknowledge that honoring the wonder of each other and the diversity of the body of Christ always means caring for each other but may also mean choosing to worship and serve separately.